CW01496138

EXPLORING
INDUSTRY

Cliff Lines

Illustrated by Stephen Wheele

Exploring the Past

Series Editor: Stephen Setford
Designer: David Armitage

Cover picture: Women workers at the Coventry Machinists' Cycle Factory.

First published in 1987 by
Wayland (Publishers) Ltd
61 Western Road, Hove
East Sussex, England BN3 1JD

British Library Cataloguing in Publication Data
Lines, C.J.
    Exploring Industry. – (Exploring the Past).
    1. Great Britain – Industries – History –
    Juvenile literature
    I. Title   II. Series
    338.0941   HC253

ISBN 1 85210 0079

Phototypeset by Kalligraphics Ltd, Redhill, Surrey
Printed in Italy by G. Canale & C.S.p.A., Turin
Bound in the UK by The Bath Press, Avon

Contents

1 Introduction

Look out of your window at the scene outside. If you live in a town, as most of us do, you will probably see houses made of brick with tile or slate roofs. Even if you live on a modern housing estate, the materials used to make the houses, and all the furniture and household goods inside, started life in a factory some time ago. The house you live in and those you can see through your window are part of the past. Some materials they are made of may already be out of date – for example, gutters and drain pipes are now made of plastic instead of metal.

Britain is a country rich in evidence of the past. We call this evidence our heritage because it has been left to us to enjoy by the people who lived here before us. Exploring our heritage can be very exciting and what we find out can help us to understand the world of today as well as how people lived in the past.

This book will show you how to explore one part of our heritage – industry, which is the making or manufacturing of goods. This will involve finding out about things that were made in the past, where they were made and the people who made them. Industry includes such activities as milling flour, mining coal, building ships and weaving cloth, as well as making the bricks for your home. Industrial archaeology is the name given to the study of places connected with the industries of the past.

In this search for the past you will be the detectives and the clues you will need are in the pages which follow.

Industry is all around us, whether we live in town or country. What evidence can you see of industry and things made in factories in the picture opposite?

What's in a name?

Are there any children in your class whose surnames are the names of trades or crafts? For example, the most common surname in Britain is Smith. This name was probably first used in the Middle Ages (about 800 years ago) because the family made metal goods such as horseshoes. In Saxon and early Norman times most people were known by a first name such as Peter or John, to which was sometimes added the name of the place where they lived, a nickname, or the kind of work they did. These second names, or surnames, were often handed down from father to son. So, for example, Richard the baker became Richard Baker.

Through the centuries the spellings of these names may have changed, but the link with the past still remains. Some crafts which were once common are rare or do not exist today. For example, a fletcher made arrows and a cooper made barrels. The surnames have survived and remind us of these crafts.

Blacksmiths can still be seen working in some villages. People with Smith as a surname once had a member of the family who was a blacksmith.

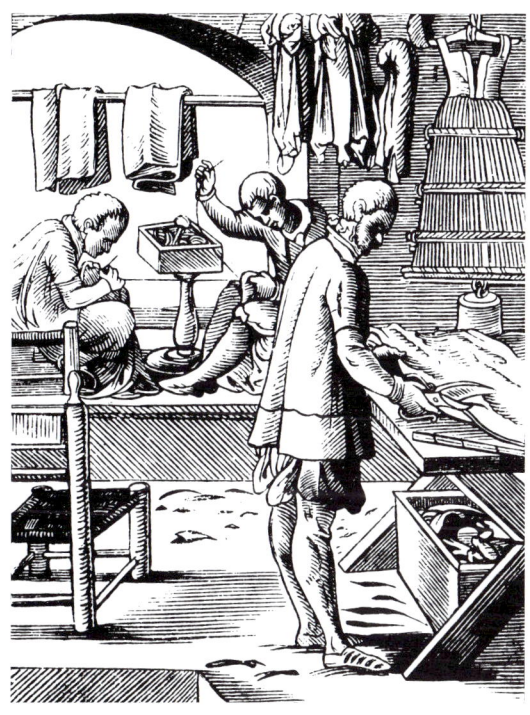 

Look at the further reading list on page 45. Some of the books listed there, which you can find in the reference section of your local library, explain what surnames mean. Find out what the following craftsmen did to earn their surnames:

turner; cartwright; weaver; skinner; mason; glover; brewer; tyler; chandler; fuller; cutler; plummer.

Which members of your class have names connected with crafts in the past? Can you think of others? Make a list of what the names mean.

Clues in your district

Is your district well known for a particular industry? Northampton is famous for its shoes while Livingston, one of the Scottish new towns, has many electronics firms. Many towns have a variety of industries grouped together on industrial estates. These estates are usually less than thirty years old and some are still being built.

Above Sixteenth-century wood engravings showing a tailor (left) and a dyer (right). *Below* Inn signs often provide good clues to the history of your area. Which industry do you think this sign relates to?

BETTLE & CHISEL

Street and road names can sometimes tell us a great deal about the past. **Above** A windmill still stands nearby but the watermill, which is also shown on old maps, has now been demolished.

Older industries grew up near rivers, canals or railways. The factories, sometimes called mills, used steam power to drive their machines and needed large amounts of coal to heat the furnaces. Many of these buildings can still be seen although they may not be making the goods for which they were once famous.

Over 200 years ago, before steam engines were invented, industrial buildings were very small. Some used water power and were close to streams, but many goods were made in people's homes or in outhouses nearby with members of the family providing the power needed to work the simple machinery.

Where are the factories in your district? You are likely to find some on industrial estates and older works near water or railways. In the countryside there may be quarries or mines. Many of the earlier industrial sites have disappeared but names like Mill Lane, Foundry road, Malthouse Cottages and Brick Hill are important clues. As you travel round your district look out for names of this kind and such things as inn signs (The Dyer's Arms), dates on walls, commemorative plaques and the remains of buildings once used by industry. The chart opposite shows you how to sketch your discoveries.

A dockland warehouse. Such buildings are used to store industrial products.

hints on sketching

You will need:

A clipboard (a piece of firm card or hardboard 30cm × 21.5cm).

A frame (a piece of cardboard 26cm × 16cm with a rectangle cut out 22cm × 12cm).

A large paper clip, bulldog clip or peg.

Several sheets of A4 paper.

A soft pencil (2B)

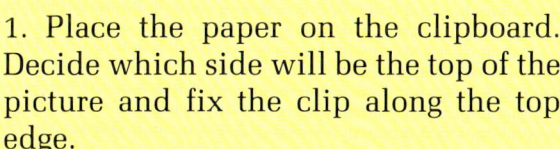

1. Place the paper on the clipboard. Decide which side will be the top of the picture and fix the clip along the top edge.

2. Hold the frame in front of you and use it to decide what to include in your sketch.

3. Sketch in the outlines very faintly, then add details and shading. Then go over the correct shapes making the lines bolder.

4. Back at home or school, go over the sketch with black pen or biro. Rub out pencil marks gently and add colours if you want. Give the picture a title, a date and write on any interesting details.

2 Industries in decline

Are any members of your family out of work? Many British shipyards, steel works, factories and mines have been forced to close because the goods they once produced are no longer wanted, or can be made more cheaply in other parts of the world. Some of the worst unemployment is in those areas where heavy industries, making bulky and heavy goods such as ships, railway engines and boilers, once prospered. The steel industry is the most important heavy industry and many steel works have closed. At Corby in Northamptonshire, for example, the steel works has been demolished and the land used for new factories.

A coal mine at Ebbw Vale, Wales. The increasing use of oil, gas and nuclear power over the last twenty years has reduced the demand for coal and resulted in many pits closing down.

Disused docks at a shipyard on the River Clyde, Scotland. Shipbuilding is one of the 'heavy' industries which have declined in recent years. These industries once employed large numbers of workers. Unemployment has been worse in areas where they were many heavy industries.

Because shipbuilding has declined, there are empty yards to be seen along the Clyde and in other shipbuilding centres such as Tyneside. Although the yards are closed many of the workers still live nearby.

As oil and gas have taken the place of coal, many pits have closed. In South Wales 25 pits stopped work between 1970 and 1984. The winding gear and buildings may still be seen as can the coal tips and workers' cottages. Some mines have been turned into museums and are open to the public. In Lancashire many cotton mills have been taken over by other industries, such as engineering, or are being used as warehouses.

Have any works in your area closed? Is there anything left to remind people of what was once there? Make a list of any industrial premises that have closed down in your area in recent years. Compare this with a list of new industries and factories that have been built over the same period – what do you notice? Make a copy of the graph below and complete it using these figures:

Year	1976	1977	1978	1979	1980	1981	1982	1983	1984
Number of ships built on the Clyde	32	17	23	23	16	8	10	16	12

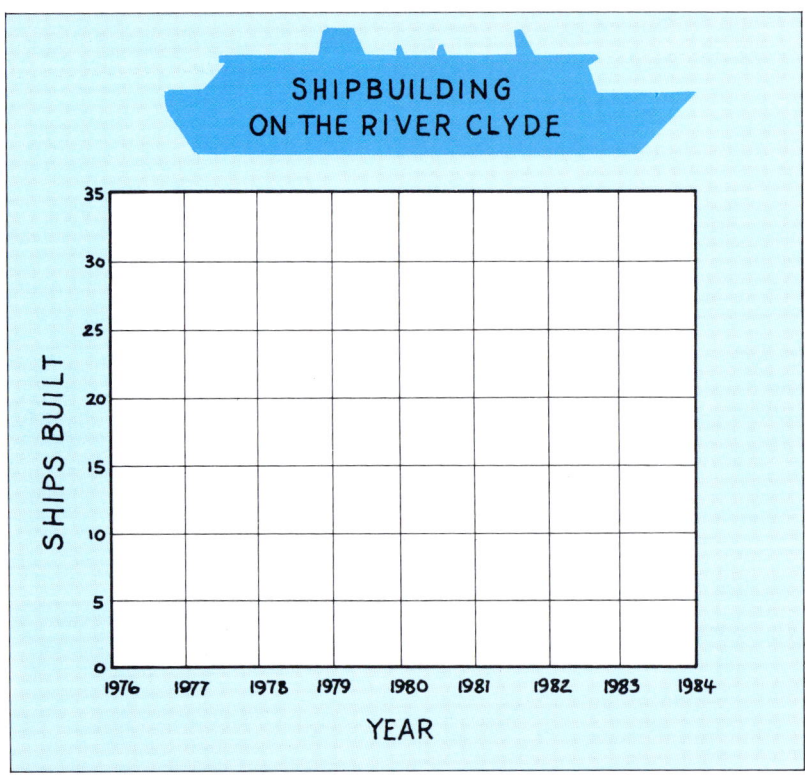

Make a similar graph to show the changes in the number of mines producing coal in South Wales:

Year	1975/ 76	1976/ 77	1977/ 78	1978/ 79	1979/ 80	1980/ 81	1981/ 82	1982/ 83	1983/ 84
Mines producing coal	44	43	39	39	38	36	36	35	30

12

3 | Food and drink

When you eat a plate of baked beans you are eating processed food. The beans have been through a number of processes in a factory before they reach the shops. Food processing is usually done in large factories using conveyor belts, but in the past it was a small-scale industry.

One of the earliest foods to be processed was the herring. For hundreds of years herrings were salted and stored in barrels. Smoking herrings over a fire probably started in the 1830's at Yarmouth in Norfolk. If the herrings were split open and smoked they were called kippers (keepers), or bloaters if they were smoked whole. Scottish Loch Fyne kippers and Arbroath Smokies (smoked haddock) are sold overseas as well as in

An old engraving of herring-curing at Yarmouth. What do you think each of the people in the picutre is doing? (Read the description of kipper preparation overleaf.) How much do kippers cost today?

Britain. Here is an old fisherman describing how kippers are made:

'Take freshly landed herring, gut them, and soak them in brine (salt water). Wash off the salt and put them on sticks, 30 to a stick. Hang them in the curing house over a fire of oak logs. How long you leave them there will depend on the weather; they need several hours to dry and about 12 hours to smoke. They used to sell for a penny each.'

Look for old curing houses made of brick in fishing ports. You may also be able to find old photographs of curing houses. Photographs are always valuable clues about the past. Other clues to look for in connection with food and drink are:
- old bakeries (often still in use in some villages)
- old breweries (usually in small towns or cities)
- oast houses (round brick buildings in the countryside where hops were dried)
- cider presses (used in the West Country to crush apples and pears)
- old distilleries (once common in many parts of the Scottish Highlands)

Tape record someone who has worked in a food or drink factory describing their job.

Above Demonstrating how a nineteenth-century cider press works, at a museum of rural life in Somerset.

Below These oast houses have now been converted into a chapel.

4 The Industrial Revolution

The Industrial Revolution, which started about 1760, was a period during which many types of machines were invented to be driven by steam power instead of by humans, horses or water. Furnaces burning coal produced the steam and since many machines could be driven by one steam engine, large buildings, called mills or factories were built to house them. Factories grew up near coalmines and people left the countryside to live close to these factories. As a result towns quickly developed; Birmingham, for example, had 23,000 people in 1731 but by 1831 it had ten times as many.

These houses show how cramped living conditions were for working class families.

Terraced housing of the Industrial Revolution, with a back alley running between the rows of houses and a factory close by.

15

Many of our towns and cities still contain a great deal of evidence of the Industrial Revolution. Look for such things as old factory buildings, tall chimneys and waste tips. The workers' homes are usually rows of terraced houses with the front door opening onto the street. They often have small backyards leading out to a narrow alley. You will find many of the buildings have been darkened by layers of soot from the factory chimneys; that is why the region around Birmingham is sometimes called the 'Black Country'. Many of these houses have now been completely modernised, with electricity and proper bathrooms and lavatories installed.

Look at the plan below. List the ways in which this house is below the standards we expect today. Make a similar plan and list for a house built in the nineteenth century in your district.

Look for the large houses built by the factory owners and merchants. They are not usually in the same parts of the town as the workers' homes.

As you can see from the plan below, workers' houses were very simple, with none of the luxuries which we enjoy today.

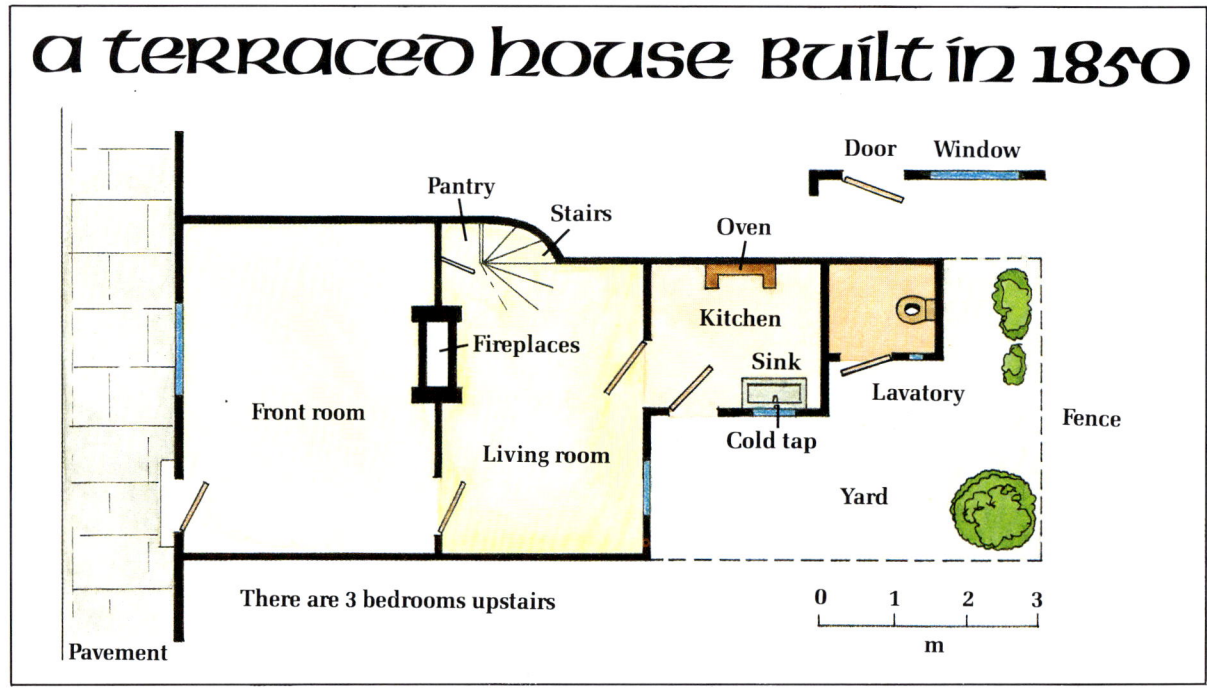

a terraced house built in 1850

Door Window

Pantry
Stairs
Oven
Fireplaces
Kitchen
Sink
Front room
Lavatory
Fence
Living room
Cold tap
Yard
There are 3 bedrooms upstairs

0 1 2 3
m

Pavement

5 The cotton industry

The mills

The first cotton mills were built at Cromford in Derbyshire in the 1770's, using water from a local stream for their power. Few people lived where the mills were built and advertisements for workers were put in local papers. The mill owner was Richard Arkwright, who invented cotton machinery. He had to build houses for the workers and some of these can still be seen. Arkwright became rich and built a castle nearby for his family.

A few kilometres away Jedediah Strutt built several mills at Belper in Derbyshire. A number of mills were also built in Scotland; the best known are at New Lanark where a planned village, a school and an 'institution for the formation of character' were built.

The New Lanark project in Scotland, built by Robert Owen. In contrast to many mill owners, Owen tried to pay his workers a fair wage and refused to employ children.

As steam power replaced water power to drive the machinery, cotton mills were built on the coalfields in Lancashire and in the Glasgow-Paisley region. Mills of different ages can still be seen and these clues will help you to recognize them. Early cotton mills are four to six storeys high. They are narrow buildings with sloping roofs and widely spaced windows. There may be a date over a doorway and a chimney stack which will have been added later.

Cotton mills of the mid-nineteenth century and later are very much bigger. They are box-like with flat roofs, tall chimneys, rows of rectangular windows and a tower. Both early and later mills were built close to water but for different reasons.

Are there any mills in your district? Sketch or photograph them and write brief accounts of their history.

The Quarry Bank Cotton Mill in Cheshire. This mill is now preserved as a working museum, where visitors can see how mill workers used to live. Some mills were fine examples of architecture, although conditions for the workers inside were often appalling.

A mill in Rochdale, Lancashire. Many old mill buildings can be seen today, although some may now be used for different purposes, such as warehouses.

Working at the mill

Documents and newspaper articles which you may find in your local library tell us what life was like in the cotton mills. From advertisements we know that children aged seven and over were employed by Richard Arkwright. Work went on day and night with two shifts of workers each working twelve hours with a break of an hour in the middle. The only day off was Sunday when the children went to Sunday school and their parents to church.

The Strutt mills at Belper kept records of people who broke factory rules and had to pay a fine out

A cartoon showing the exploitation of children in the cloth trade. Children worked in mills, mines and factories from the age of six or even earlier. For the employers they represented cheap labour; for their parents, the small income they brought in often made all the difference.

19

of their wages. The table below gives details of what some of these offences involved:

Offence	What had been done
Leaving mill without permission	Going to Derby fair
Damaging mill property	Stuffing a stove tunnel up
Not working properly	Leaving her machine dirty
Misbehaving outside working hours	Rubbing their faces with blood and going round the town to frighten people

The mill owners organised parties for the workers. At Arkwright's mills in September there was a 'candle-lighting' ceremony. Workers paraded round the village with a band and went back to the mills for buns, fruit, beer and nuts.

Below is a young mill girl's diary for one day in September. She earned 3 shillings (15p) a week. Write a diary of what you do and what you eat on a typical Monday.

Monday 24th September ∘1830∘

5.30 a.m.	Get up
5.45 a.m.	Walk to work
6.00 a.m.	Start work, fined if late
8.30 a.m.	Breakfast break, make tea and eat bread and butter
8.45 a.m.	Return to work
1.00 p.m.	Dinner break. Eat bacon and potato pie
1.30 p.m.	Return to work
5.00 p.m.	Tea break, make tea eat apple and bread and butter
5.15 p.m	Return to work
8.30 p.m.	Finish work and go home
10.00 p.m.	Go to bed.

Left *How do you think you would cope if your day was as long and tiring as the mill girl's? What do you think of the food she had to eat? How does it compare with your diet?*

6 Iron and steel

Are there any cast iron covers set into the street where you live? Look for such things as manhole and drain covers, gratings, post boxes, foot scrapers and old lamp posts. They may show the date and place where they were made.

Iron goods have been made for over 2,000 years using iron ore and charcoal, but it was not until the eighteenth century that large quantities of iron could be made by smelting the ore with coke. Abraham Darby found that iron made with coal was of a poor quality. He then discovered that if the coal was first heated to give off its sulphurous fumes, the cinders left (called coke) could be used in blast furnaces to melt iron ore without spoiling the metal. His furnaces at Coalbrookdale in Shropshire are now part of the Ironbridge Gorge Museum which is well worth a visit.

Above An old water-pump outside a church. Look for such cast-iron relics in your neighbourhood or local museum.

Below The world's first cast-iron bridge was built in Shropshire. The place where it stands is now called Ironbridge.

making a wrought-iron pattern

You will need:
A soft pencil (2B).
A pad of A4 paper.
Scissors.
Several sheets of thick card.
Coloured wax crayons.
(see also 'Hints on sketching', p.9.)

1. Sketch a wrought-iron pattern from a fanlight, coal-hole, cover railing, balcony or similar street features.

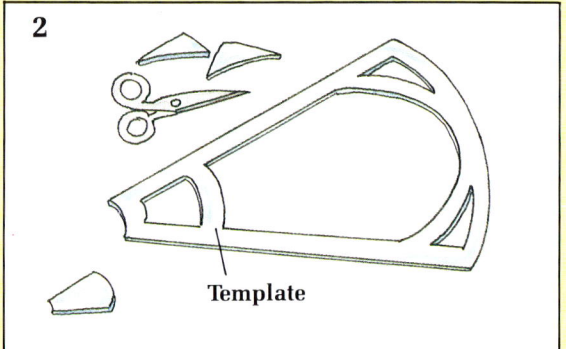

Template

2. Make a design from part of the pattern. Draw it on card and cut out a template.

3. Use the template to make your own design for a bookcover, table mat or frieze. Add the details from your original design and either leave it in black and white or add colours. Take rubbings of your template with wax crayons.

Water power (and later steam) was used to work the furnace bellows and drive the heavy hammers needed to shape the white-hot iron. Near Coalbrookdale is the first bridge in the world to be made of iron. The sections of this bridge were cast at Coalbrookdale and assembled in 1779.

Iron furnaces were built of brick and stone where coal and iron ore were near at hand, but only a few have survived. There is one at Moira in Leicestershire and others at Neath Abbey in West Glamorgan.

Steel

Steel is much stronger than iron because impurities such as carbon have been removed from the metal. In the eighteenth and early nineteenth centuries small amounts of steel were made in furnaces by heating iron in sealed clay pots called crucibles. Because it is hard, steel was used for making tools needing a sharp edge such as swords, knives and some farm implements.

Large steel plants were built towards the end of the nineteeth century after the invention of the Bessemer Converter and open-hearth furnace. In recent years the demand for steel has fallen and many works have closed. In nearly every case the sites have been cleared and used for other purposes. If you live near a place which once had a steel works, make a survey of the works as it was and collect pictures of what the plant looked like. Try to find out what it was like to work there.

A steelworks near Glasgow – many such works have closed and the sites been redeveloped in recent years. It is important that records are kept of these factories and what it was like to work there.

7 Using clay

Bricks were made by hand before machinery was invented to do the task. Clay dug from a pit was hosed with water to remove impurities. It was then put through a mixer and pressed into a mould. The mould was made of wood and shaped like a shoe box with no lid or bottom. After the clay blocks had been left to dry under cover or in a shed, they were stacked in a kiln. A furnace of wood or coal was lit under the kiln and the bricks were baked for several hours. They were removed from the kiln when cool.

Brickmaking by hand in Essex, 1888. The brickmaker (centre) is shaping lumps of clay in a wooden mould. Behind him, his mate is stacking the shaped bricks onto a barrow to take to the kiln for firing.

Shaping, or 'throwing', clay on a potter's wheel to make ornamental vases. The wheel is powered by hand, while the woman in the centre of the picture weighs out the correct amounts of clay for throwing.

Brick works were once common in many parts of the country where clay was plentiful. They can often be seen on nineteenth-century maps. Clues to look for in the countryside include brick rubble used to make paths to the site, the foundations of old brick buildings and overgrown clay pits. Old brick works, quarries and mining sites can be very dangerous places. Keep outside fenced areas, look out for warning notices and always take a grown-up with you who knows the area well.

During the Industrial Revolution the making of pottery using a fine white clay, called china clay (kaolin), flourished in Staffordshire, Worcestershire and a few other places. Men like Josiah Wedgwood became famous for their porcelain and some of the early bottle-shaped kilns they used can still be seen. By looking at the bases of porcelain cups, saucers or plates you can often find the maker's name. Look for small workshops in your district where potters make mugs and similar goods for sale to tourists and craft shops. If possible, join a local pottery class to learn how clay is shaped and fired today.

Brick kilns at Stoke on Trent, Staffordshire. This part of England is known as The Potteries because it has traditionally been the centre of the industries using clay.

making miniature bricks

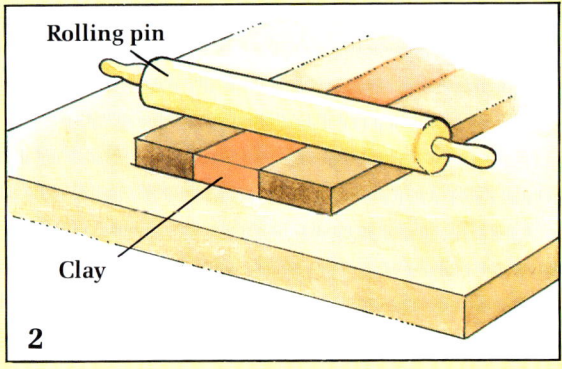

Guide lines 4.5cm apart — 15cm — 27cm — 30cm — 1.5cm — 3cm — 2.5cm

1

You will need

A block of balsa wood approximately 30cm × 15cm × 2cm.

Two thin strips of balsa wood 27cm × 3cm × 1.5cm.

Nuclay (or similar material).

Glue.

A rolling pin.

A pencil.

A knife.

1. Glue the thin strips of wood to the larger block, 2.5cm apart. Mark lines 4.5cm apart across the strips of wood.

2. Pack Nuclay into the space between the wood strips. Use an old rolling pin to make the clay the correct thickness.

3. Carefully cut the clay into stips 4.5cm long, using the lines marked on the strips as a guide.

4. Remove the bricks from the mould. Make another set of bricks. Use your bricks to build the patterns used on buildings and walls in your district. Why are these patterns used? What names are given to these patterns, or 'bonds', as they are also known.

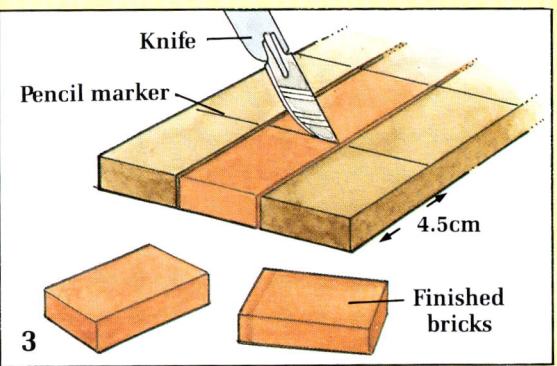

Rolling pin

Clay

2

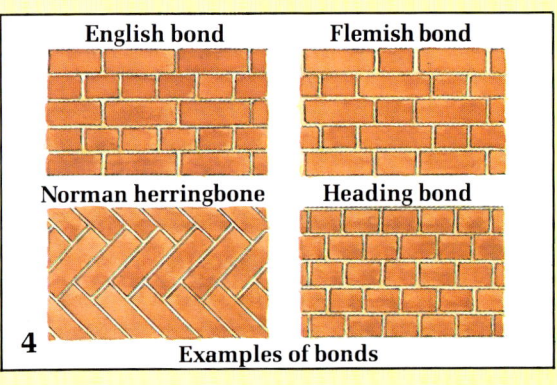

Knife

Pencil marker

4.5cm

Finished bricks

3

English bond · Flemish bond · Norman herringbone · Heading bond

4 Examples of bonds

8 | Quarrying

A disused lime kiln at Upper Wharfedale in Yorkshire. In the eighteenth and nineteenth centuries lime was used mainly for agricultural purposes; today, lime is an important building material.

Is the roof of your house tiled with slates? Slate was an important roofing material from the end of the eighteenth century until about 50 years ago. It came from quarries in the highland regions of western Britain. Houses in Glasgow and Edinburgh were roofed with slate from Easdale and Ballachulish in Argyll, while North Wales provided slate for many English and Welsh homes. Some slate quarries are still working, although they are not as busy as during the Industrial Revolution because clay tiles are made more cheaply in factories.

You can still visit the quay at Port Penrhyn on the Welsh coast, where ships were loaded with slates from Penrhyn quarry to carry round the coast to towns such as Bristol and London. The port declined when the railways were built and took over the trade. Near the quarry is Bethesda, which grew up as a mining village with a hospital for the quarry workers and their families. The quarry was owned by Richard Pennant, who

The slate quarry at Dinorwic, Wales, dates back to Victorian times.

27

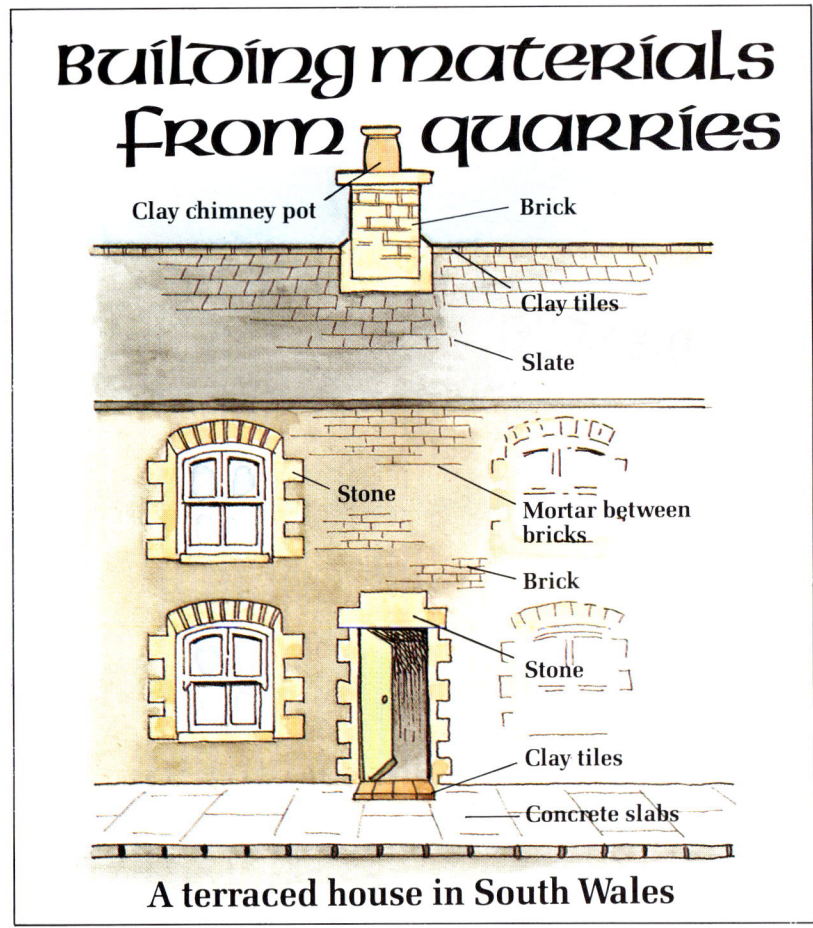

Building materials from quarries

Clay chimney pot — Brick

Clay tiles

Slate

Stone

Mortar between bricks

Brick

Stone

Clay tiles

Concrete slabs

A terraced house in South Wales

Some of the building materials to look out for which originate from quarries. Building materials may differ slightly in your area, depending on where you live. Look at more modern houses – can you identify the materials used? Are they much different from those used in houses built at the turn of the century?

became Lord Penrhyn. His home, Penryhn Castle, is owned by the National Trust and contains a museum with many relics of the slate industry.

Another building material which comes from quarries is lime, used in making mortar and cement. To make lime, limestone or chalk is heated in large kilns and many early kilns (like those at Middleton in Midlothian) can still be seen today.

In your district there may be quarries producing sand and gravel, building stone or china clay. Find out about them but remember that they are dangerous places to explore. Make sketches like the one above to show the building materials used on houses in your district.

9 Mining

Many coalmines have closed in recent years and in some cases the surface buildings, winding gear, tips and railway sidings can still be seen. People who worked down these mines may still live nearby in miners' cottages and families may have sons, fathers and grandfathers who have been miners. The stories these people can tell about their experiences as miners or miners' wives are well worth tape-recording. Prepare your questions carefully beforehand. Write them out and focus each one on a particular point, such as, 'What did you wear down the pit?'

You can also find out what it was like working in a coalmine in the nineteenth century from reports made by inspectors and commissioners. Newspapers often carried details of local mines and pit disasters and these accounts may be in your public library or in a mining museum.

Young women carrying coal up ladders in a Scottish mine. From the Royal Commission Report on the Employment of Children in Mines, 1842.

The empty shells of engine houses at Botallack in Cornwall are all that remain of the old tin mines.

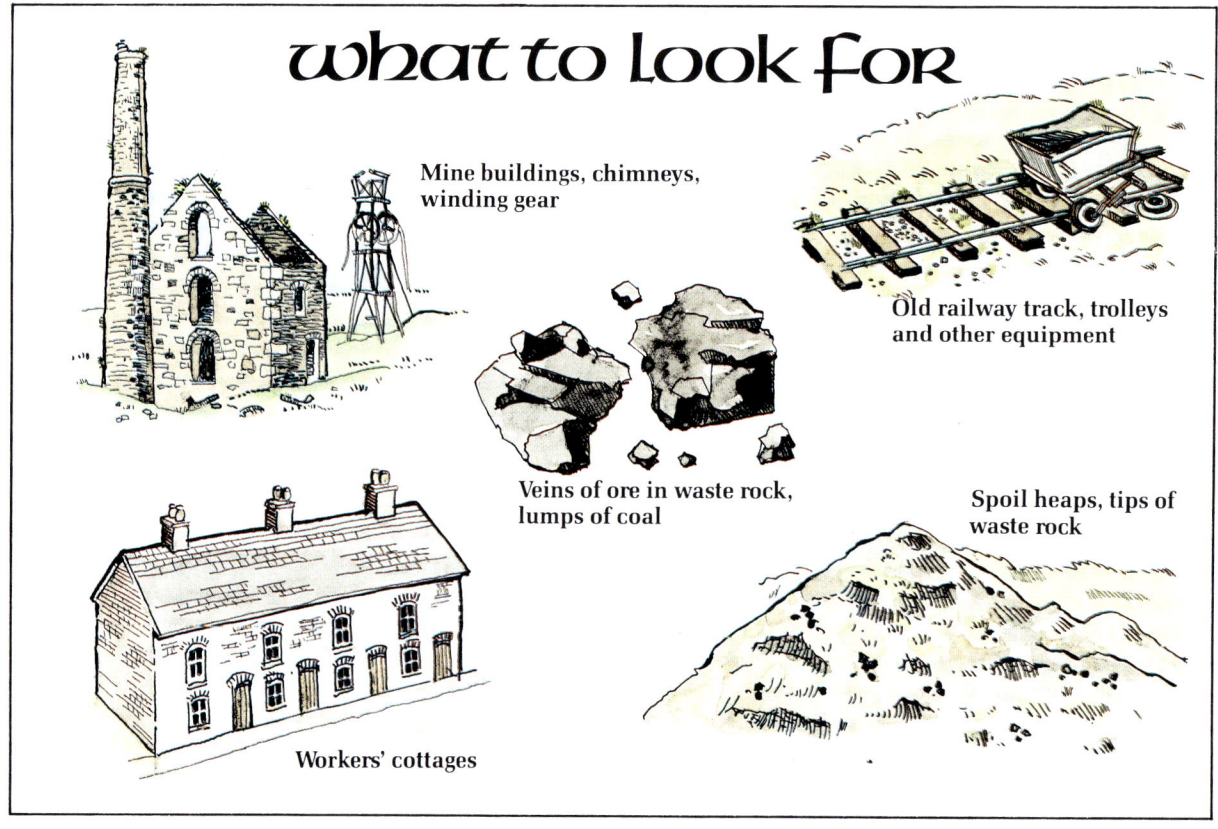

what to look for

Mine buildings, chimneys, winding gear

Old railway track, trolleys and other equipment

Veins of ore in waste rock, lumps of coal

Spoil heaps, tips of waste rock

Workers' cottages

The sketch on page 29 was drawn for a report in 1842 on women and children in the mines. Among its conclusions the report stated that 'Children are taken into these mines to work as early as four years of age ...' The report also noted that in the east of Scotland many of the people employed were girls: '... the chief part of their labour consists in carrying the coals on their backs up steep ladders.'

If you live in a coal mining district, or such counties as Cornwall, where there are old tin or copper mines, or Derbyshire where lead was important, look for local relics like those shown above. Trace the outline of the British Isles from a large map in an atlas. Find out the main areas of coal mining in Britain and mark them on your map. Also add the principal areas for mining other minerals such as tin and copper.

A few items to look for when visiting a mining area.

Post mill

Smock mill

Tower mill

10 Before steam

Wind and water power

The two main sources of power before the steam engine was invented (other than human or animal power) were the wind and running water. Both forms of power were used to turn a series of wooden wheels and cogs which drove machinery. Most windmills were used to grind corn into flour and a few worked pumps to drain the surrounding land. Windmill designers had to solve the problem of how to turn the sails and some of the machinery connected to them towards the wind.

In the earliest windmills, called post mills, a massive upright oak post supported the body of the mill which was suspended so that it could rotate around the post. Later smock mills were built shaped like a farm worker's smock. They had a wooden frame but only the top section of the mill, called the cap, turned. Tower mills were built of brick or stone with a wooden cap. The cap turned into the wind by means of a fantail.

Windmills can be found in many parts of the country. They appear on old maps and are also marked on the 1:50,000 Ordnance Survey maps (Second Edition) sold in bookshops. Look for windmills on high ground or, in the wetlands near drainage ditches. In a few places, modern versions of windmills are today used to generate electricity.

When you visit a windmill make a note of its type: post, smock or tower. Sketch or photograph it and look around outside for old millstones or pieces of machinery. Many old mills are open to visitors and once inside look for the machinery

31

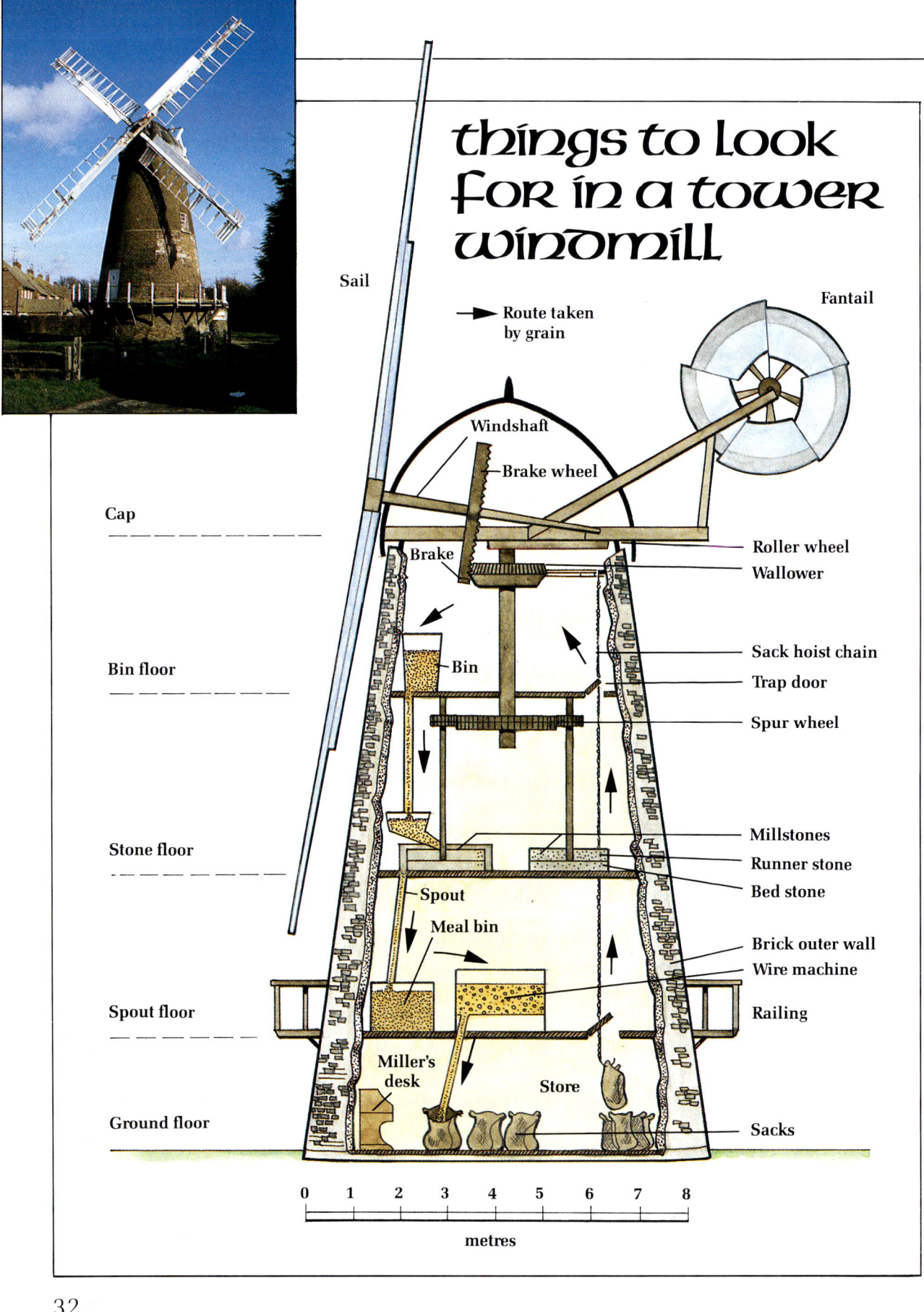

things to Look for in a tower windmill

Sail

Route taken by grain

Fantail

Windshaft

Brake wheel

Cap

Brake

Roller wheel

Wallower

Bin floor

Bin

Sack hoist chain

Trap door

Spur wheel

Stone floor

Millstones

Runner stone

Bed stone

Spout

Meal bin

Brick outer wall

Wire machine

Spout floor

Railing

Miller's desk

Store

Ground floor

Sacks

0 1 2 3 4 5 6 7 8

metres

shown on the diagram overleaf. Do not be put off because there is more machinery than the diagram shows. Try to find out about the miller, where he lived and what he was called.

Watermills

Watermills were used to drive machinery in Britain long before windmills were built. At the time of the Domesday Survey in 1086 there were over 5,600 watermills. At first they were used for grinding corn but later the water-wheel drove a variety of machinery. It could move a hammer up and down to full cloth (beat it in water to tighten the weave). Hammers were also used to grind dyes and shape iron in the early iron foundries. You may discover when you visit the site

Left *Some of the features to look out for when you visit a tower windmill.* *Inset* *Polegate windmill, East Sussex.* *Below* *Typical watermill features.* *Inset* *The seventeenth-century watermill at Rossett, Wales.*

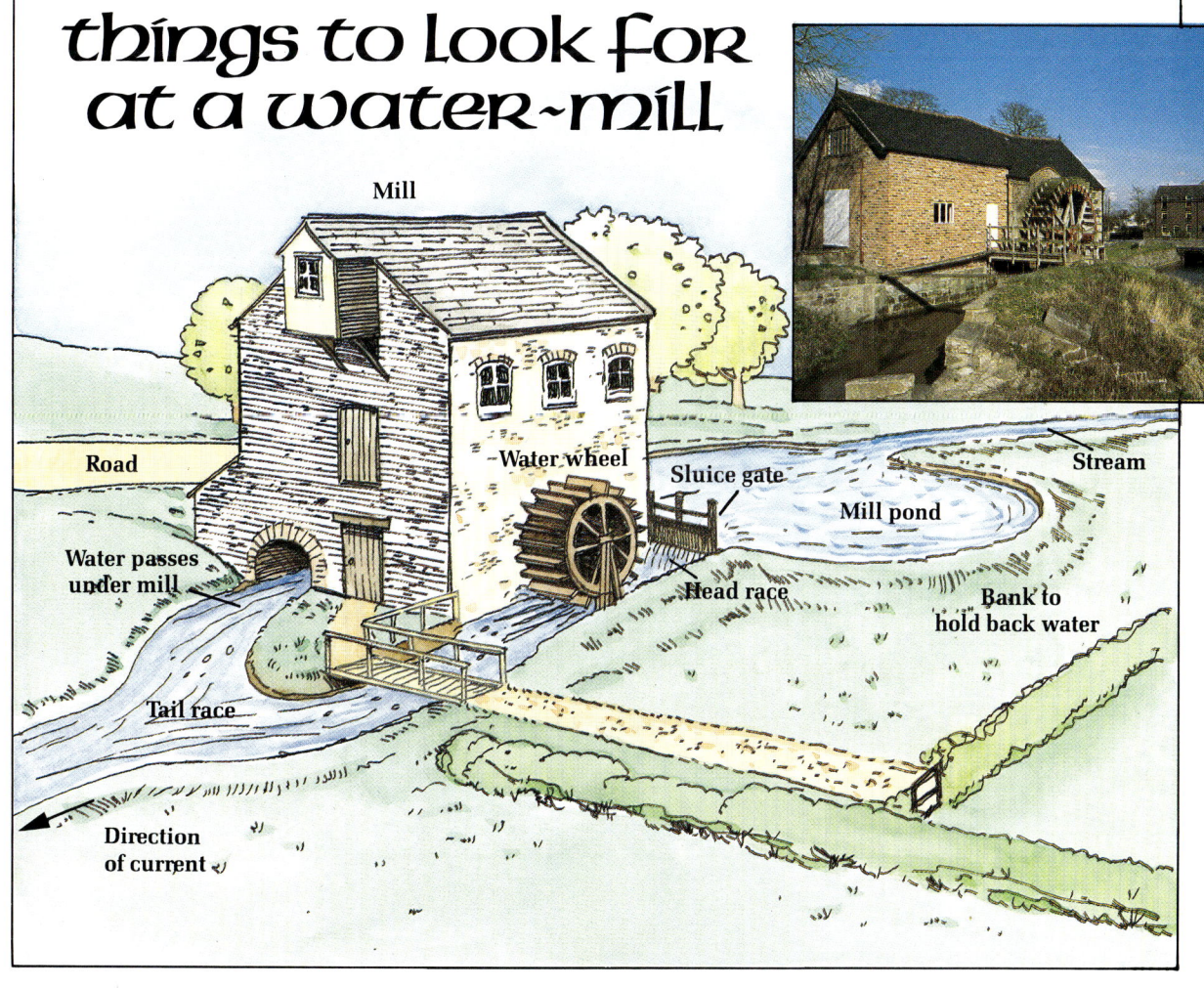

things to look for at a water-mill

Mill

Water wheel

Road

Sluice gate

Stream

Mill pond

Water passes under mill

Head race

Bank to hold back water

Tail race

Direction of current

that some of the features, such as the wheel, have gone. The things you should look for are shown on the diagram on page 33. If the stream was fast-flowing there was no need to build a dam to form a mill pond and control the flow of water. The wheel could be turned by the force of the water and was called an undershot wheel.

A better and more reliable method was to dam a stream to make a mill pond and then position the wheel so that the weight of water falling into the buckets turned it. This is called an overshot wheel. Sometimes you will see breast wheels where the water fills the buckets half way up the wheel. Some watermills are grinding corn once more for sale to shops and visitors. Today, we have hydro-electric stations which use the power of fast-flowing water to generate electricity.

When you visit a watermill, make a note of the type of water-wheel used. Carry out your own experiments into powering a water-wheel following the instructions opposite.

types of water-wheel

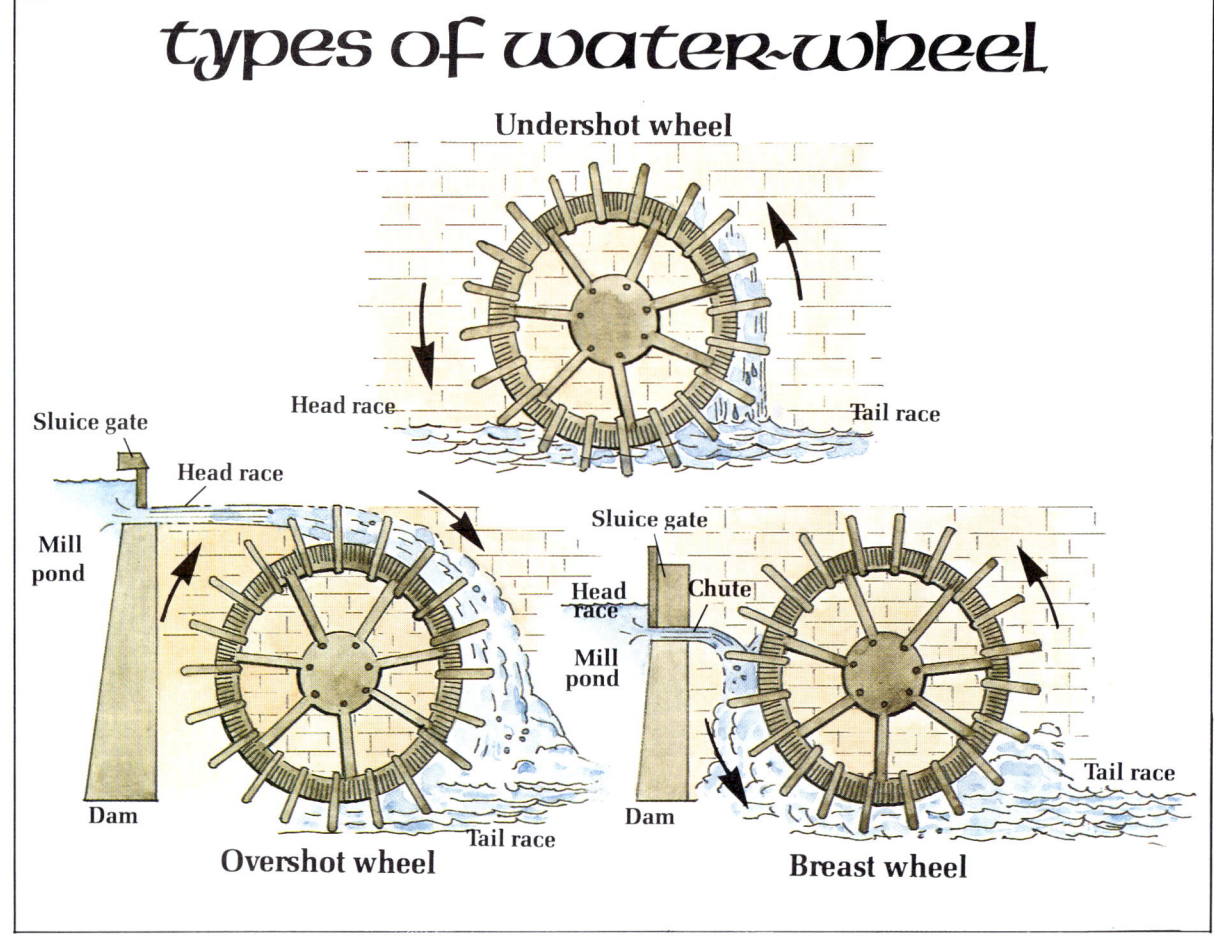

Undershot wheel

Head race   Tail race

Sluice gate

Head race

Mill pond

Sluice gate

Head race

Chute

Mill pond

Tail race

Dam   Tail race

Overshot wheel

Dam

Breast wheel

making a water-wheel

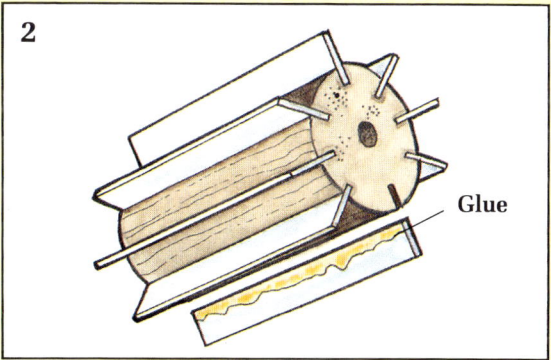

1

Hole

Slot

Slot

You will need:

A cork with straight sides.

8 strips of firm plastic from a detergent bottle 4cm × 1.5cm (alternatively, you could use plastic plant tags).

A piece of stiff wire 8cm long.

2 blocks of balsa wood

Glue.

Blu-Tack (or similar material).

1. Drill a hole through the centre of the cork so that the wire will pass through and allow the cork to turn easily. Cut 8 slots 3mm deep down the sides of the cork, at equal distances from each other.

2. Cut 8 strips of plastic the same length as the cork. Glue them into the 8 slots you have made.

3. Pass the wire through the cork. Stick a small piece of Blu-Tack either side of the cork. This will stop the cork sliding about. Glue the two blocks of wood together to form a right angle. Fix the wire into the centre of the upright piece of wood.

4. With your water wheel in a bowl or sink, direct a flow of water along a tube from a tap. Experiment to find at what position the flow is most effective.

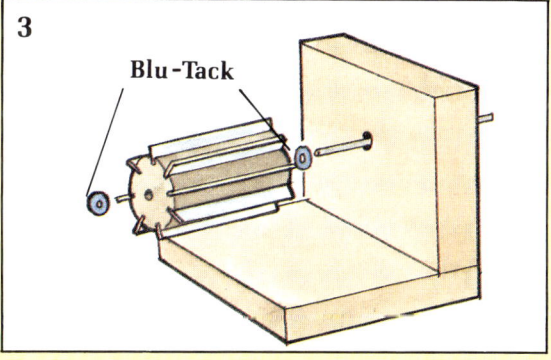

2

Glue

3

Blu-Tack

4

Tube

Water

Bowl or sink

11 The wool industry

The spinning and weaving of wool to make cloth became an important industry in parts of Britain in the thirteenth century. The most important areas were the West of England, Yorkshire and East Anglia. The industry was based on the 'Cottage System' whereby the cloth was made in the workers' cottages or in small workshops, and not in factories. Cloth merchants, called clothiers bought the wool from local farmers and sent it by pack horses to the homes of the villagers. Some families spun the wool, others had looms and were weavers while others finished the cloth. The clothier organised the work, supplied the materials and many of the tools, paid the workers and sold the finished cloth.

Fourteenth-century cottages of Flemish weavers in Lavenham, Suffolk. Skilled settlers from Flanders and elsewhere helped to make East Anglia an important centre of the wool trade.

The industry grew up where there was sufficient wool available and streams in which the wool could be washed. Human energy provided the power needed to spin and weave the cloth. One of the centres of the industry was Lavenham in Suffolk where Thomas Spring was a rich clothier. There are many relics of the Spring family including their wool mark, used on the bales of wool and cloth, and the magnificent tower of the parish church which they paid for.

Clues to look for when you visit one of these areas are the half-timbered cottages of the workers; the clothier's home; churches and family tombs; the guildhall and other buildings where the wool trade was organised.

Although most woollen goods today are mass-produced in factories, the cottage system is still used in parts of the Highlands and Islands of Scotland for producing woollen goods. The Harris Tweed orb and cross wool mark can be seen on clothes produced in this region.

Design a wool mark for your family based on the family name or your initials.

The wool mark of Thomas Spring of Lavenham.

The Guildhall at Lavenham, where members of the wool trade met to control and organize the local industry.

12 Early iron workers

Charcoal was used to make iron before smelting with coke was discovered. The iron makers needed good supplies of timber and iron ore, and streams which could be dammed so that water wheels could provide the power to work furnace bellows and the forge hammer. The main centres of the industry were in South-East England, the Forest of Dean, the West Midlands, Cumbria and Argyll, in Scotland.

At Ashburnham, East Sussex, a clock maker in the eighteenth century engraved the face of a clock with the different processes used by local iron workers. They are shown making cannon and firebacks. Iron firebacks were used to protect the brickwork in a fireplace. Here is a copy of the clock face with the hands removed. The drawings show the pond (called a hammerpond), a water wheel which would work bellows at the furnace and downstream a second water wheel working the hammer needed to beat the metal into shape at the forge.

Among the clues which can be found of this industry are hammerponds, old cottages and the houses of the ironmasters. The water wheels and

The house 'Batemans' in Sussex was once the home of a local ironmaster. It was later lived in by the writer Rudyard Kipling.

furnaces have mostly disappeared, although one has been restored at Bonawe Ironworks, Taynuilt, Argyll. Pieces of furnace clinker and lumps of iron can sometimes be found while local names to look for include Hammerbrook, Minepit Field, Cinderbank Wood and Furnace Farm. Iron cannon, cannon balls and firebacks can often be seen in museums.

The Ashburnham clockface. Write down what it is happening at each of these times: 11 and 12, 1, 2, 8 and 9, 7, 3, 4. What is happening in the four corners of the clockface?

13 The earliest factories

Some of the first workers to make goods for other people to use were the flint and axe makers of the Neolithic period (approximately 4000–1800 BC). Flint is a hard stone found in chalk in layers, and can be broken or 'knapped' into sharp-edged flakes which can be used as cutting tools.

At flint mines in Norfolk called Grimes Graves, Neolithic people dug pits into the chalk to get

Below *How a working flint mine may have looked, showing miners cutting out lumps of flint from the foot of the mine and carrying them and waste chalk to the surface.*

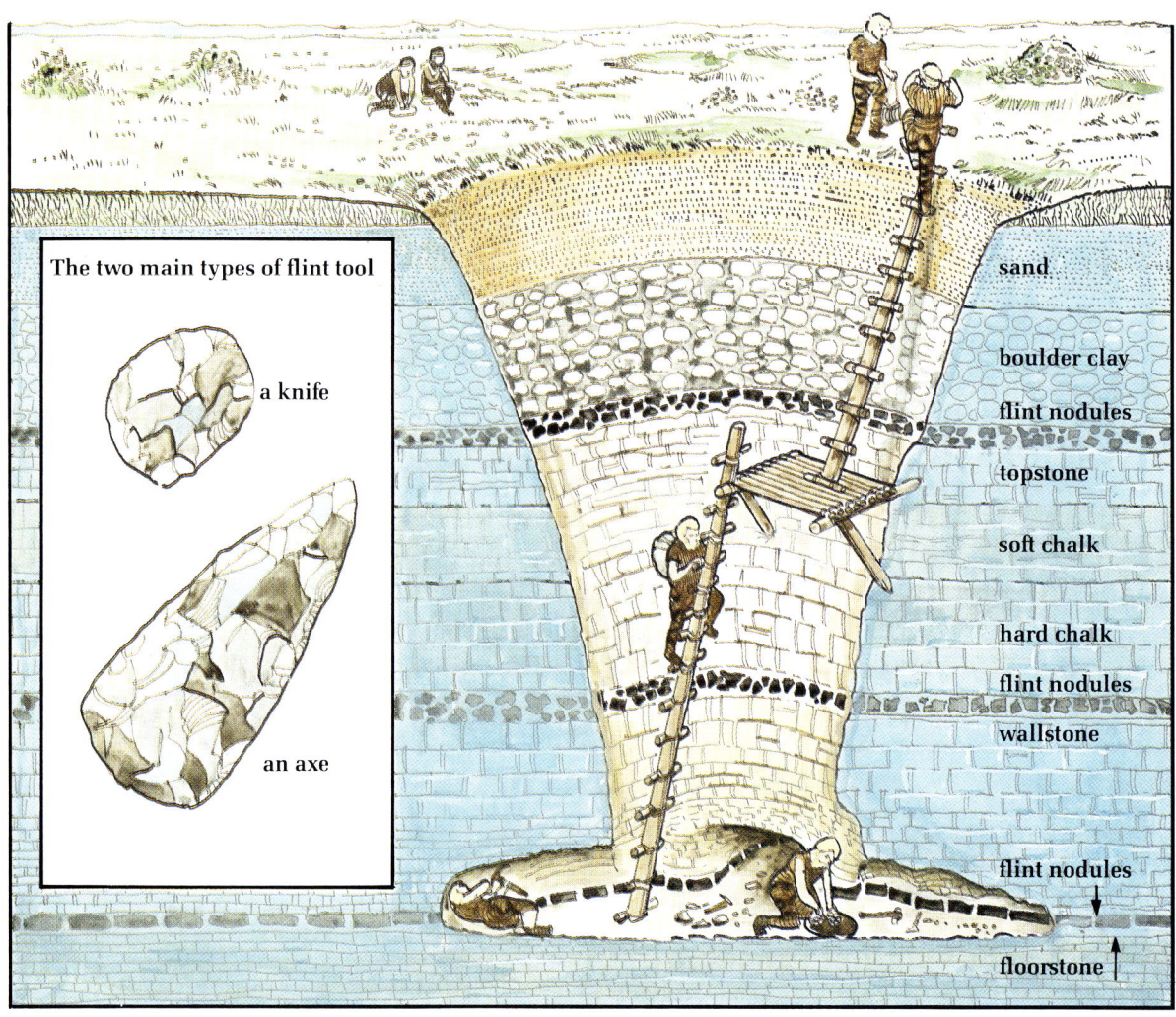

The two main types of flint tool

a knife

an axe

sand

boulder clay

flint nodules

topstone

soft chalk

hard chalk

flint nodules

wallstone

flint nodules

floorstone

out the layers of flints. They used antlers as picks and worked by the light of candles made with grease and a wick. On the surface the flint was broken up and shaped by skilled knappers. Heaps of broken flint prove that these first 'factories' were close to the mines. The flint was shaped into axe-heads, knives, arrowheads and scrapers to be traded for food and hides.

In parts of Britain where there was no flint, hard rocks were used as axe-heads. Four axe 'factories' have been traced. They were near the coast in Northern Ireland, Cumbria, North Wales and Cornwall. Axe-heads from these centres have been found as far away as London, Southampton and the Firth of Forth.

In chalk areas look around the edges of ploughed fields for sharp-edged flints. Broken flints provide naturally sharp edges. Find out what they are able to cut, but ask an adult to help you as they can be very dangerous. Visit local museums for examples of stone tools made during the Neolithic period. What stone was used? Where did it come from? Sketch these tools and add a scale to show their approximate size.

Above left An aerial photograph of Grimes Graves, showing the filled-in mine shafts, which look like bomb craters or bunkers on a golf course.
Above right The custodian of the Grimes Graves site gives a demonstration of flint knapping.

14 A local project

Now is the time to show just how good a detective you are by using the clues in this book. By now you should know something about industry in your district, but there is much more to be discovered. Do not be too ambitious in your choice of a topic for a local project. A history of industry in your district would probably fill an encyclopaedia! Choose a very limited topic such as the history of one factory, the life of a mining family in the 1930s or an industrial trail to show visitors the places and objects connected with industry in one part of your town or local area. To record what you see and hear the essential equipment is a clipboard, paper and pencil, a copy of a local map and some coins to use in photocopiers. Also very useful are a camera, tape recorder and a measuring tape.

Research your topic in a scientific manner by first observing, then recording and finally interpreting and presenting your discoveries:

Observing   In this first stage you should use your eyes to look around at buildings and sites and find out what information is available in libraries, museums and private collections.

Recording   Photograph or sketch the site; make measured drawings; talk to old people and record their answers to your questions; collect information from books, newspapers and maps. When you photocopy material or copy an extract from a book always make a note of the author, book title, publisher, publication date and page number.

In organizing your local project on industry, you may find it helpful to use the example opposite as a guide.

42

organizing a local project

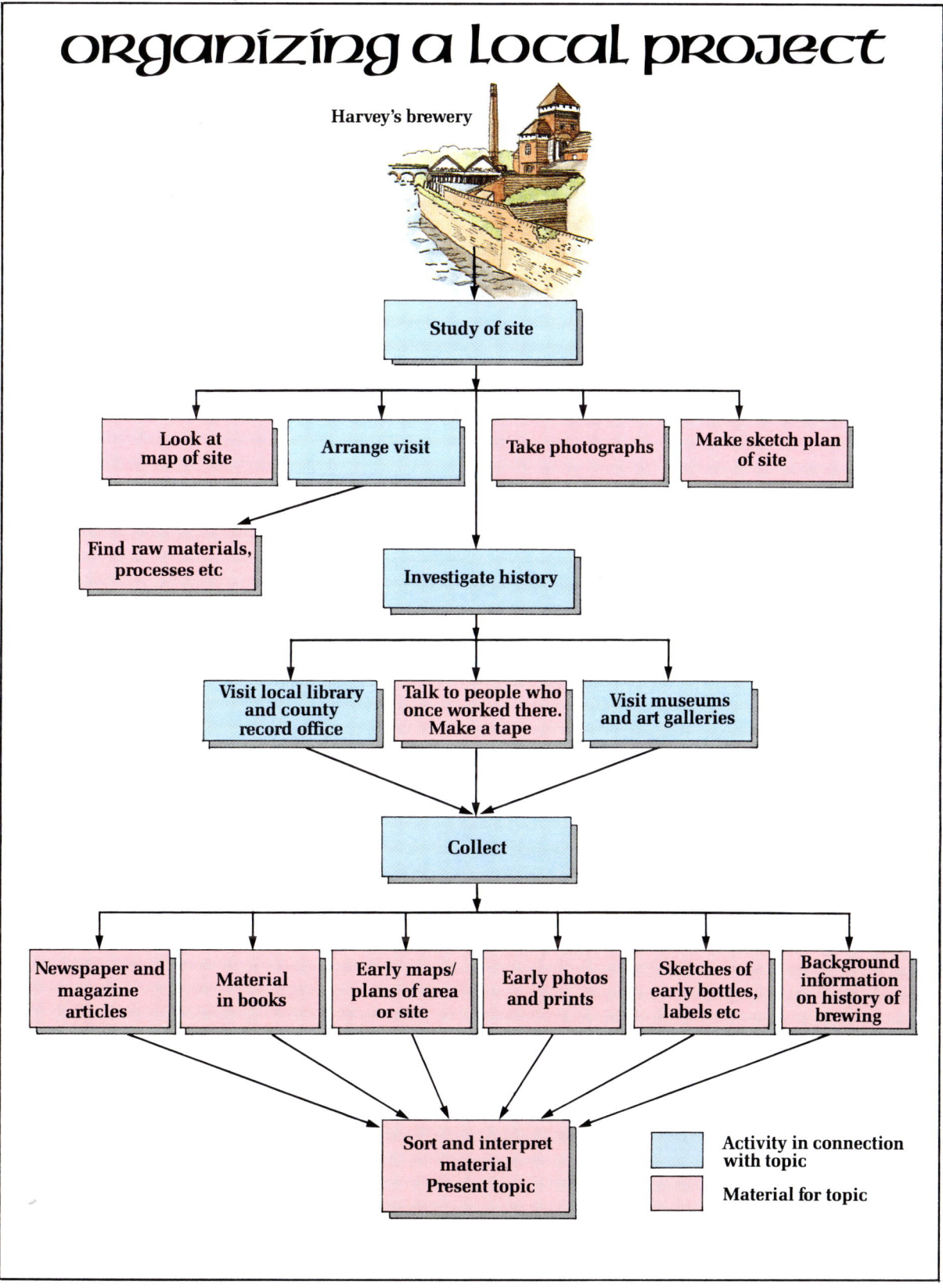

Harvey's brewery

Study of site

- Look at map of site
- Arrange visit
- Take photographs
- Make sketch plan of site

Find raw materials, processes etc

Investigate history

- Visit local library and county record office
- Talk to people who once worked there. Make a tape
- Visit museums and art galleries

Collect

- Newspaper and magazine articles
- Material in books
- Early maps/ plans of area or site
- Early photos and prints
- Sketches of early bottles, labels etc
- Background information on history of brewing

Sort and interpret material Present topic

Activity in connection with topic

Material for topic

Interpreting and presenting   Look through your material and ask yourself such questions as why the site was chosen and what were the important events in the firm's history. Also decide how the work is to be presented (a loose-leaf file is a useful form) and – this is very important – what material you have collected is essential and what should be left out of the finished topic.

The future

In the past many historical relics and industrial buildings have been pulled down because the land was needed for other things. Now we are beginning to realize that industrial relics are part of our heritage and should be conserved. Volunteers spend part of their spare time on conservation projects. What is there in your district connected with industry and in danger of being destroyed which should be conserved? Do other people agree with you? Form a Conservation Club at your school to get more support and make local councillors and planners aware of your concern.

Sources of information

There are three ways in which you can obtain material for your topic. You can use your eyes to find local evidence, you can talk to people and you can use documentary evidence, most of which can be found in libraries. Many libraries have local studies sections and there are County Record Offices in most county towns.

Local directories   Some go back 200 years, they show the names, occupations and addresses of local people.

Local histories   The Victoria County Histories, published about 1900, are a useful source. Old newspapers – advertisements and articles in local newspapers can be very useful although it can

An old windmill stands in front of a modern power station. One of the best ways to begin gathering information for your project is to use your eyes. Look around you for evidence of industry in the past – especially for the contrast between old and new industrial buildings.

take a long time to sort through past issues unless you have a year and date as clues. Early copies may be kept in the newspaper's offices.

Local history books   These often tell you a great deal about churches and nothing about industry! Many books were written about wind - and water mills and recently specialist books on industrial archaeology have begun to appear.

Maps   Large scale Ordnance Survey maps such as the 1:2,500 show and name factories, mines and quarries. The earliest Ordnance Survey maps (first edition, 1:10,560 and 1:2,500) were published between 1805 and 1873. These have been reprinted in recent years and may be in your local library. Old street maps can also be useful.

Photographs   These are far better as accurate sources of information than paintings or etchings.

Further Reading

Allen, Eleanor, *Industry* (A & C Black, 1977)
Bracegirdle, B., *The Archaeology of the Industrial Revolution* (Heinemann, 1973)
Cossons, Neil, *The BP Book of Industrial Archaeology* (David and Charles, 1975)
Harris, Nathaniel, *Spotlight on the Industrial Revolution,* (Wayland, 1985)
Hassall, W. O., *History through Surnames* (Pergamon Press, 1967)
Hennessey, R. A. S., *Factories* (Batsford, 1969)
Reaney, P. H., *A Dictionary of British Surnames* (Routledge & Kegan Paul, 1976)
Vialls, Christine, *Windmills and Watermills* (A & C Black, 1975)
In addition, David and Charles publish a series of books dealing with the industrial archaeology of a particular county, region or industry. Two examples are: Ashmore, O., *Industrial Archaeology of Lancashire,* and Butt, J., *Industrial Archaeology of Scotland.*

B.

BADDELEY, William furgeon, High ftreet
Salton, Richard, grocer and chandler, ditto
Bannifter, Jof. baker, ditto
Banton, James, weaver, ditto
Barlow, widow, ditto ditto
Bate, Thomas, fadler, ditto
Bate, Benjamin, maltfter, Hampton ftreet
Bathew, John, mercer, High ftreet
Bennet and fons, ironmongers, New ftreet
Benfon, Jofeph, dyer, Hampton ftreet
Blews, Lewis, padlock maker, High ftreet
Bourn, Jof. grocer and chandler, High ftreet
Bourn, Myles, mercer, ditto
Bradney, Samuel, currier, Hall ftreet
Brinton, Stephen, butcher, High ftreet
Bunn, Richard, maltmill and bellows maker, ditto

An extract from the 1780 directory for Dudley, in Worestershire. You may find similar directories for your area in your local library. Some of the occupations and the printing of the letter 's' (which looks more like an 'f') may seem strange to us.

Glossary

Bessemer Converter A large steel vessel used to make steel from pig iron by removing impurities.

Charcoal Wood that has been charred: that is, heated in a container or a sealed mound so that it does not catch light and burn.

Clothier A merchant who organised the purchase of wool and the making and selling of cloth.

Coke Coal which has been heated in an oven to remove chemicals, such as sulphur, which are given off as a gas.

Conservation The care and protection of the environment for the future.

Cottage system The making of goods for sale in the homes of the workers or in nearby outhouses. This method of production was used before the factory system was introduced.

Curing house The brick or stone building in which fish are dried and smoked over an oak fire.

Distillery A place where liquids are converted into alcohol, e.g. the manufacture of whisky.

Fantail An automatic device for turning the cap of a windmill into the wind. It consists of a series of wooden blades forming a wheel-shape which are set at right angles to the sails. The wind turns the fantail and forces the cap round.

Fireback A block of cast iron placed at the back of a fireplace to protect the brickwork.

Forge The building in which metal is shaped by being heated and then hammered.

Guildhall A building owned by the members of a medieval trade association and used as a meeting place. These associations or guilds controlled particular trades such as the manufacture of woollen cloth.

Hammerpond A large pond formed by damming a stream to control the flow of water driving a water wheel. The name comes from the heavy hammer powered by a water wheel which was used at an iron forge to beat the metal into shape.

Heavy industry The manufacture of goods which are heavy and bulky when compared with other goods, e.g. iron and steel, shipbuilding and boiler making.

Heritage Something which has been inherited.

Industrial archaeology   The study of buildings, sites and other evidence of industry in the past.

Industrial Revolution   The development of steam power and the invention of different types of machinery after about 1760 which resulted in Britain becoming the leading industrial country in the world.

Iron furnace   The building in which iron ore is heated until it becomes a liquid, loses some of its impurities and can be poured into moulds to cool.

Knapper   A person who breaks up and shapes stones.

Mill   1. The building in which textiles such as cotton and woollen goods are made. 2. The shortened name used for a windmill or watermill.

Neolithic period   The period from about 4,000 to 1,800 BC, when farmers using stone tools lived in Britain.

Oast house   A building designed so that hops can be dried in a kiln and then stored before being used to flavour beer.

Open-hearth furnace   A container in which molten iron is poured and then converted into steel by the use of a draught of air to remove impurities.

Processed food   Food which has been prepared by a number of processes before it is sold. Processing in a factory results in the food requiring far less preparation at home before it is eaten.

Scythe   An agricultural tool used for cutting grass or cereal crops. It consists of a wooden handle fitted with a long, curved steel blade.

Sluice   An artificial channel for water, with a sliding gate for controlling the flow or direction.

Smelt   To heat ore until it melts, leaving behind most of its impurities.

Warehouse   A building in which goods are stored.

Watermill   A building in which the machinery is driven by a water-wheel.

Water-wheel   A wheel containing buckets or paddles which is turned by the force of running water.

Winding gear   The wheel and other mechanical parts on the surface of a mine which are used to raise and lower cages in the mine shaft.

Windmill   A building in which the machinery is driven by the wind turning sails.

Wool mark   A symbol stamped on wool and wool cloth to show the maker or place of origin i.e. a trade mark.

Index

Picture Acknowledgements
The publishers would like to thank the following for supplying pictures: British Tourist Authority 21 (bottom); English Heritage 41 (left and right); Mary Evans Picture Library *cover*, 13, 15 (top), 17, 19 (bottom); Hutchison Library 8 (bottom); C.J. Lines 8 (top), 21 (top), 32 (inset), 37 (bottom), 38; The Mansell Collection 29 (top); TOPHAM 7 (bottom), 11, 14 (top and bottom), 15 (bottom), 18, 23, 24, 25, (bottom), 27 (bottom), 33 (inset); Simon Warner 5, 19 (top), 27 (top); Steve Wheele 9, 12, 16, 20, 22, 26, 28, 30, 31, 32, 33, 34, 35, 37 (top), 39, 40, 43; Zefa 6, 10, 29 (bottom), 36, 44. All other pictures are from the Wayland Picture Library.